Forex Technical Analyses and Fundamentals

Smit Chacha

INTRODUCTION

Forex trading in currency or oil market is profitable, however still many lose money in forex business. I will teach in this book how to maximize your profits in the forex industry. I will point out all the possible pitfalls that you should be careful about as well all the uptrends that you need to know for profitable forex trading.

Forex is risky business and a newcomer can easily lose lots of money in a single trade. Many traders lose money in forex, even the more experienced ones. But forex is profitable and you can make a full time living with forex.

I will show you how to manage your money in multiple trades and transactions so you can split your profit and losses. I will also guide you in how to pull off a trade and how to recover your losses.

And finally, I will teach you how to make full time income as a forex trader. I will highlight all the best forex brokers and the weekly/monthly economic calendar news that you should be aware off.

This book is about how to combine forex technical analyses and fundaments for profits. Most traders use either technical analyses or plain fundamentals when doing traders, we will combine both for better profitable forex trades.

Let's do forex!

CONTENTS

Is Forex for you

If you purchased this book then you are probably in to forex or thinking in doing forex. The next question is do you want to do currency exchange as a full time or part time. It is easy to make a living with forex with a limited fund. If you want to live a life seating at home, watching television (news) and spending most of your time in front of a computer or a smart phone then forex may be the ideal job for you!

Making a living in forex means to keep track of daily news events worldwide. These are the fundamentals of forex and it can drastically change the value of a currency in just a few seconds of a breaking news. This means if you want to profit in forex you must be prepare for any drastic fluctuations (volatility) in the currency market.

Keeping a track in the daily events makes a huge difference while profiting in the stock market. Politics, business events even the weather and time plays a critical role in the stock market. Forex market as you know are open 24 hours Monday to Friday and during this time there will be lots of volatility in the market.

Every day of the week new events will raise not only on the economic calendar where most of the agenda is pre-booked but there will be also breaking news events that will conflict your daily forex agenda. This is why fundamentals plays the most part in the currency volatility. Missing a news event and only counting on what the economic calendar is a mistake that can lead to profit losses.

In forex and general stock market news is everything! Missing or not keeping a track of it can lead to big losses which can take time to overturn. Keeping track of the news will ensure that your profits keep raising on daily bases. In forex depending on the margin that you set up you can still lose money. Having your positions open overnight can lead to variable interest charges set up by your broker. Ideally you want to close a position before the closing trading hours of the day while netting your profits. And this can only be archived by keeping the track of the daily news events.

In short anything doing with the economic calendar, politics, news and so are called Fundamentals and they play a big part in forex. Other is Technical Analysis which we will talk later on. But for now, what you should know is that Fundamentals plays 80% part in daily forex while the remaining 20% is Technical Analysis.

TECHNICAL ANALYSIS VS FUNDAMENTALS

Most people find technical analysis or fundamentals the key of success in forex, they are 2 different things and combining both together is the key for success.

We will get more into detail on each of them in later chapters but for now I want you to keep in mind that you need to combine these 2 things together to predict what will happen next.

Another thing to keep in mind is the sentiment of which the market is heading towards. There are many tiny variables to keep in mind when doing forex.

These tiny movements in the market can cause huge losses and gains, it all depends how well are you tracking the currency market.

In short technical analysis is viewing the tiny changes that happens on the graph and fundamentals is what is going on in the world (news, calendar). Combining these 2 things will define your success in forex.

Most people find technical analyses sufficient to drive gains in the market, however the market will fluctuate or will be very volatile when something happens in the news. This short volatility will change the graph in long term.

Volatility simply mean the movement that happens in the market. A high volatile market means there are lots of ups and downs, a low volatility means there is little movement in the market.

There are certain things in the calendar that defines a huge volatile market, we will get that in details in later chapters. For now, just keep in mind that the trader sentiment, fundamentals and technical analysis defines how market will react.

Keeping track of these short movements will define your overall success in the currency market.

Forex Trading: Introduction

I have been trading forex (mainly on EUR/USD) for a number of years and I have no qualifications in economics. This shows that you do not need a degree in order to do forex trading. I have been doing this full time and so can you!

I will guide you throughout the whole process in how I

trade forex. Let me emphasize that this is my method of doing forex trading. There are loads of other ways that people trade. The method share in this book is how I do trade in forex business.

Forex in profitable but there is risk involve, I will guide you in how to do risk management and how to minimize risk in your trades. Forex is a risky business, no matter how safe you trade there is always a risk of losing money. (Keep that in mind). I suggest you only invest what you can afford to lose.

With limited capital you can do profitable trade in the EUR/USD market, but as I said earlier there are risk involves. You can lose money. My method is profitable but not risk free. I have lost money in the past but my overall trading experience was profitable and I have been doing this for a number of years.

I had full time job before and I was doing forex in my spare time. After grasping an effective method of doing trade I started doing forex for full time (5 days a week). This profitable method that I use for forex trading is what I am teaching in this book. If you want to do forex part time or full time this book will guide you in doing profitable forex trades.

Forex is a 24 hours market this means you can trade Monday to Friday at any time. So, if you are working full time you can trade on this 24 hours market on your spare time.

When I started doing trades, I used to watch every trade several times a day, now after grasping a method I only do 3 to 4 trades per account a day and make at least £100+ a day. Sometimes I lose money or should I say my trades are carry forward, which means I have to pay an interest (a small amount) for my trades to be carry forward for the next day. This can happen to anyone as the market is not predictable. There are loads of variables that come to play while trading the forex market.

S&P500, Crude Oil Market and High Volatility

Crude oil market is index in S&P500 indices and is a number that you should take a fair consideration for. Crude Oil Market is where the money is, it is very volatile higher than medium indices. Forex is very volatility is low. Trading in these 2 or 3 markets will definitely be profitable. Generally speaking, high volatility is where is risk comes in, <u>only trade what you can afford to lose</u>.

Risk management is another good chapter that I will tackle later on. Your trading size matters and keep a good stopping distance. <u>Only trade what you can afford to lose</u>. I want to highlight this twice, because trading on stock market majority of people lose money!

Another good point to look for is where can you afford to carry on your trades, as some markets will triple your interest causing more loss on your pocket. Look at the previous trends and do a simple Fibonacci it is a technical analyses tool that most traders use to predict that recent future of the market trend.

Always keep an eye on breaking news, as this is where the volatility will change drastically! For example, when Donald Trump was elected the volatility of EUR/USD range from 1.16 to 1.03!

Forex XAU (Gold) and EUR/USD Volatility

If you are trading currency mainly EUR/USD consider taking a look at the gold or XAU volatility as many traders found that whenever XAU (gold) is high Dollar or USD is down and vice and versa. This is not always the case as some studies suggest that whenever there is a breaking news this hypotheses breakdown.

Keep an eye on breaking news and on XAU as well, whenever trading EUR/USD. German yields and US yields also matters in how to trade currency on the long run. Do regular Fibonacci to predict recent future of the market trend.

Trading EUR/USD is a profitable and the same time risky as many traders lose money on the forex market. Forex is a low volatile market compared to oil or indices, however that does not mean that it is a risk-free market. Only trade what can you afford to lose.

Trader sentiment suggest that whenever the market is bullish or bearish studying the trend where the market will crossover will make you a profitable trader.

What are Technical Analysis Fundamentals

Generally speaking, technical analysis is a formula to calculate short term market prediction. Where the market trend is heading. The formula that most traders use of Fibonacci. Measure the graph from bottom to top for each recent market trend.

Fundamentals is where the volatility becomes in, all the breaking news and microeconomics calendar. In later chapters I will tell which significant monthly and weekly calendar days you must be aware of. For instance, every Friday on first month nonfarm payroll report data is published and market volatility is very high for EUR/USD. There are many others I will tackle those in later chapters with examples.

Technical Analyses How does it Work

Technical analyses simple means watching and studying the graph, the pattern of the graph, where the graph is heading ahead. And there are time frames that you can check.

For example, let's say in a 5 minutes time frame the candle stick gone up, in the next 5 minutes time frame where does the candle stick go? Will it go further up, same level or down? If in the next 5-minute time frame the candle stick goes up, it means that in that time frame the market is heading in an uptrend or bullish signal. Same for the downtrend or bearish signal.

Now that does not mean that it is a bullish signal for the whole day, for instance the time frame of 15 minutes chart could suggest a different story. It is very much possible that the 5-minute time frame the candle stick suggest a bullish trend, but in the 15-minute chart it could suggest a downtrend.

Same applies to a daily chart. A daily chart is where you can calculate the Fibonacci and find where exactly the market trends is heading. Or should I say where the volatility of the market will be for the following day.

My point is that keep checking the 5 minute, 15 minute and daily charts when it comes to technical analyses.

These 3 candle sticks are the most commonly used. But you can also check the 4-hour chart and so forth.

Technical analyses only predict the short-term future of the market, the longer term comes with Fundamentals. This is what decides where the volatility of the market will be. The further ups and downs of the market trend. And that is the economic calendar.

Combining both technical analyses and fundamentals you will become a Forex trader.

Fibonacci how does it work (Graphs and Examples)

Below is how Fibonacci works on Investing.com EUR/USD chart

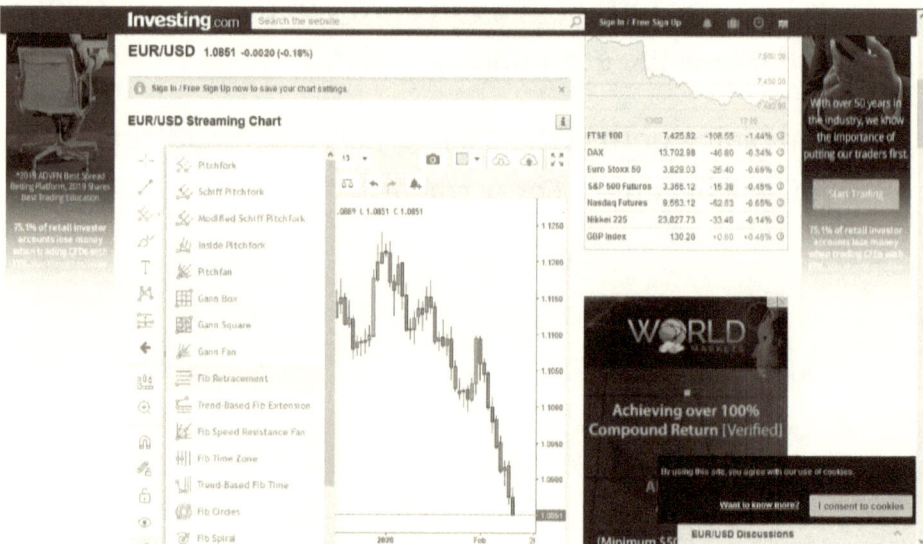

As you can see, I used the tool Fib Retracement and changed the graph to Japanese candles and in 1-day market movement from 15 minutes.

The lowest was on 2017 compared to today February 13 2020, so I retrace Fibonacci for timeframe backdated to 2017 when the market movement was similar to todays.

So, the Fibonacci for current trends would be:

Between 1.0824 (a break below this would target 107.54 and lower) to 1.0880 (a break above would go toward 1.0919).

This is how you calculate Fibonacci current trends for short term market predictor, it is a tool that the most often used as per technical analyses of the market trends. It predicts how much the market will fluctuate during the 24h trading period.

Fundamentals and Economic Calendar

As per fundamentals you must take a look on the weekly economic calendar and there are certain weekly and monthly reports that keep the market volatile, such as: Nonfarm Payrolls, Monetary Policy reports, CPI reports, etc.

You will notice that whenever there is a change in the government department such as change of presidents or any government body the market volatility will be very high for that short period and this volatility will drive the market ahead.

For instance, when Donald Trump was elected the market volatility for EUR/USD was so high that it went from 1.16 to 1.08 and lower in just a few minutes.

Even though currency market is the lowest volatile market when government bodies are in play the volatility extends drastically.

Oil market is medium volatile and reports such as oil stocks makes it more volatile for short term and this also drives the market ahead

Breaking news also drives market volatility too much, for instance recently the corona virus spread that happen in china (2020) cause the EUR/USD market to lows as 1.08 from 1.12 and oil market from 54.37 to lows as 49.57.

Fundamentals are the root cause of market volatility while technical analyses play its part the majority ups and downs happen at market fundamentals, although these are short term, they drive the market forward making it long term.

Fundamentals are seen as long-term market movers while technical analyses are seen as short-term market predictors.

Combining Technical Analyses and Fundamentals

As you can see the fundamentals for this week are (you can find the weekly economic calendar from this URL: https://www.fxpro.com/trading-tools/forex-economic-calendar).

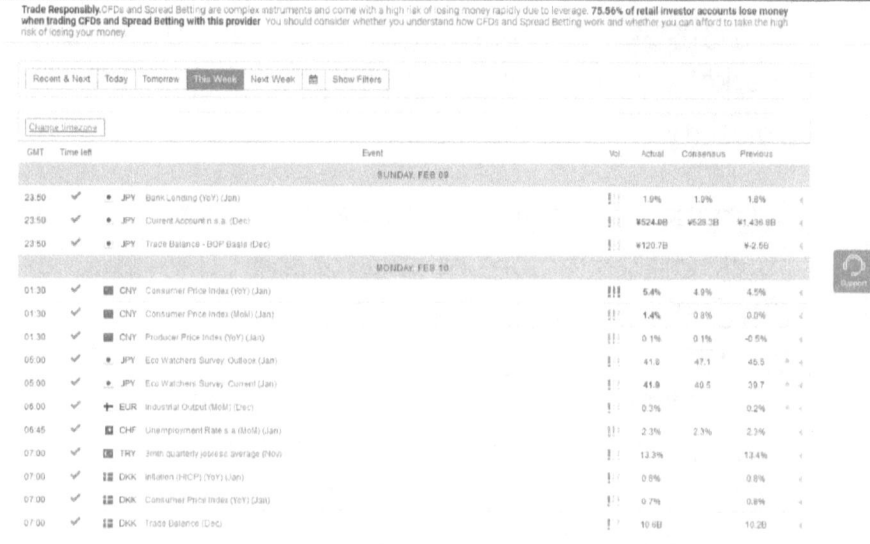

On Thursday 13 February 2020 at 13:30 pm we will receive CPI reports and they are positive which means the USD will be strong at that time.

And the graph confirms that:

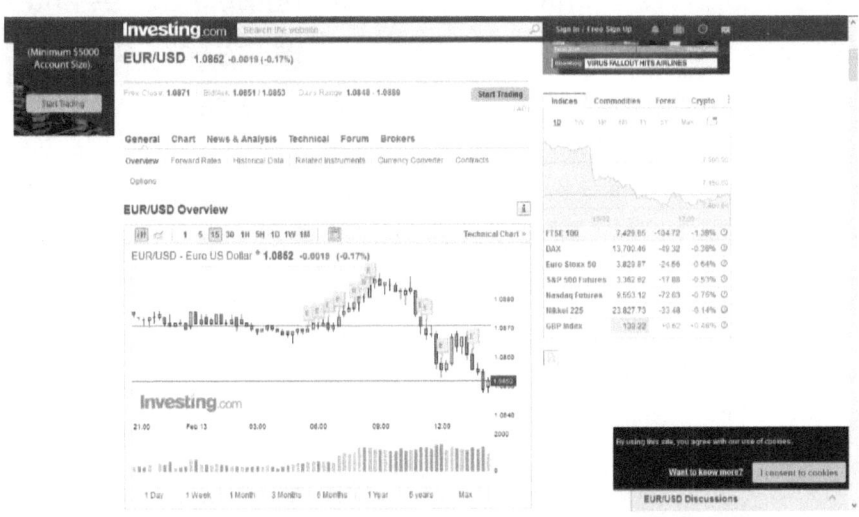

As you can see from the fundamentals of the weekly economic calendar the CPI report made the EUR/USD market to be very volatile from the moment the CPI reports where published. The market drops 0.15% since then.

Stop Loss (Normal, Guaranteed and Trailing)

When comes to trade there are certain things you can do to manage your losses, a stop loss is required in any trade and my advice is to have a large stop loss and a small size instead of a small stop loss and multiple trades.

The reason why I am suggesting a larger stop loss and a small amount of trades is because from personal experience you will lose less in long term. While others prefer to have a small stop loss and multiple trades and closing those trades before losing. This is a technique that many do and from personal experience you will end up losing more money in long term.

There are 3 types of stop losses:

- Normal
- Guaranteed
- Trailing

A normal stop loss means you can enter the amount or the point away from the market and minimize your losses, the problem with a normal stop loss is that when the market is closed and when it opens, if there is a large amount of volatility the normal stop loss may end up losing more money then you first enter it.

If you want to make sure that you never lose money than you should always use a guaranteed stop loss, this way the point away that you entered are always the amount that you are willing to lose. It puts a cap even if the market opens with a large volatility.

A trailing stop loss means the point will trail in favor of your trade. If you will end up winning more or if the market volatility favors your stop loss if will trail.

I recommendation is always to use a guaranteed top loss. I personally for EUR/USD I use a guaranteed stop loss of at least 10 cents or 1000 points with a size of 0.5 and a limit of 13 points, so my winning will be at least £6.5 per trade. For oil I use similar stop losses 1000 points a size 0.25 and a limit of 13 points. This is how I do trades.

I can afford to lose 1000 points per trade and if required I can afford to deposit further and edit the trades for my favor. I personally do not do multiple trades with a small stop loss. I prefer a larger stop loss and a minimum amount of trades.

Below is an example:

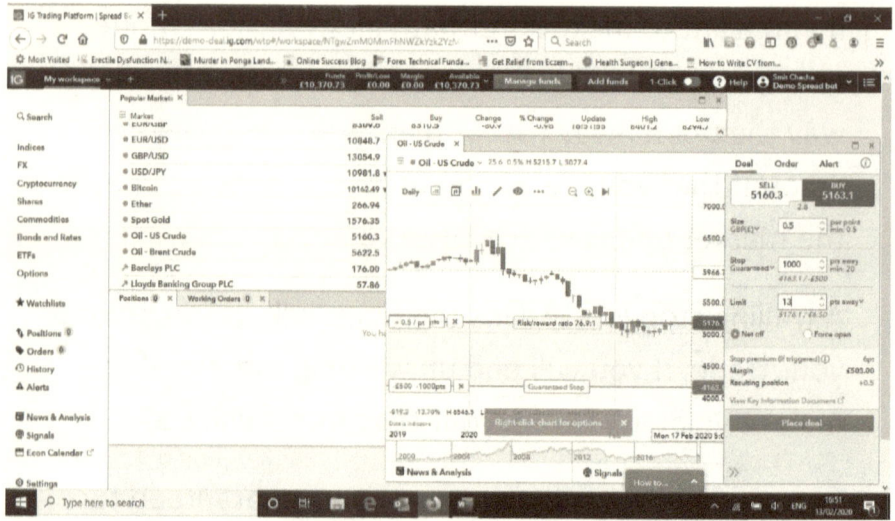

Margins and Sizes

As the new European law there is a 50% margin call for any trade you perform, meaning the margin that I choose if it drops below 50%, I end up losing 50% of my deposit. The trade will close automatically. This is a new law that started in 2019.

As I indicated earlier My advice is always a larger stop loss and the minimum size per trade. The amount of trades will vary from the amount that I am willing to lose. This way I am always safe in how much I can afford to lose.

The profits will end up to be limited, however I am confident that I will never end up losing more than what I can afford.

The rule of thumb is always avoiding redeposit to retrace your trade losses.

How to Trade Positively and Profitably

In order to make profit in the forex business you need have a serious eye on market trends and breaking news. You need to be updated with the latest trends and economic issues around the globe. Even changes in government bodies will cause drastic market movements. Panda medics and virus spreads such as corona virus made the market go downwards in 2020. President Trump elections made the currency market or should I say the USD stronger.

In order to trade positively and profitably you need to be prepared for the upcoming trend or breaking news and trade accordingly. This way you will make lots of profits the forex business.

The technical analyses will help you predict the short-term market movement for the day trading period which is done by the Fibonacci tool. This is easy to calculate, what makes huge profits is when you can combine this and fundamentals together.

And for that you need to be updated with the latest news, trends, and breaking news online and offline. There are many handy websites that I recommend visiting and keeping an eye on it and these are:

- https://www.fxstreet.com/
- https://www.investing.com/
- http://30rates.com/
- https://www.dailyfx.com/sentiment
- https://www.fxpro.com/trading-tools/forex-economic-calendar

the fxtreet.com, investing.com and dailyfx.com contain a section about the daily breaking news and reports that are constantly updated. I recommend the above websites to keep on track with the latest fundamentals report and analyses.

The Trader Sentiment

The trader sentiment in any market (currency, shares, commodities, etc.) is essential to look at. It tells you how many traders are trading in which side of the market, is the sentiment bullish, bearish or mixed.

A bullish sentiment will indicate the most traders are finding the market to go further up, while a bearish sentiment the opposite.

Generally speaking, whenever the trader sentiment is over 90% the market will go towards that trend. For example, if EUR/USD trader sentiment is bullish and 90%

of traders are on long, the possibility of the market going further up is good. However, that is not always the case, since the market is driven by a number of variables.

The fundamentals and the technical analyses must be performed with the trade sentiment in mind. In order to do profitable trades.

From my personal experience, I am not saying that this is the standards of trading. But my experience suggests that whenever the market sentiment is over 90% the traders tend to lose money. The supposed bullish trend turning mixed or even bearish for short term is possible.

I remember when EUR/USD was 1.09 and the trader sentiment was over 90% bullish and still the market went the opposite direction.

Keeping the trader sentiment in mind is a good way to find the market trend but it is not sufficient information to make a positive trade. You need to keep track of the fundamentals and a good memory of the past trends or should I say the technical analyses must be present.

Forex Spread Betting Brokers (Resources and Advice)

There are loads of forex spread betting brokers in the

market, below is a list of a few:

- IG
- City Index
- Saxo
- Plus500
- Forex.com

There is a good website with loads of reviews of each forex spread betting broker:
https://www.investing.com/brokers/forex-brokers

Choose your broker and start investing in the forex spread betting market. **Note:** majority of people will lose money, only afford to invest what you can afford.

Start with a small size and a large margin, for instance: start doing forex on EUR/USD in a smallest size with a larger margin with a guaranteed stop.

Size of your investment simple means how much you will lose or gain per point that will fluctuate. Margin is till which point you can afford to keep the position open till it is automatically closed with a loss. You can always edit the margin by depositing more money in your account.

A guaranteed stop will ensure that you will never lose more money when there is a high volatility in the market.

Keep in mind forex is a low volatility market, indices are medium volatile market while cryptocurrency is a high volatile market. Start with forex first and if you find comfortable doing spread betting feel free to invest in other commodities such as metal, oil, gold, silver, etc.

Remember what drives the market is the fundamentals or should I say that economy calendar. Keep checking for breaking news this is where the highest volatility of the market rises.

Technical analyses will help you to predict near term future of the market. **Note:** most people lose money when the volatility of the market is very high (fundamentals).

List and Reviews of the Best Forex Brokers

There are hundreds if not thousands of forex brokers out there, my preferred one is IG and this is the broker that I use to trade most often. Anyhow below are a list and reviews of the top 7 forex brokers and they are:

- IG (Best)
- CMC Markets
- OANDA
- London Capital Group (LCG)
- XTB (X-Trade Brokers)
- Forex.com

- Papperstone

IG Group

In my opinion this is the best forex broker out there, with the best online ratings and an easy to use online and mobile platform. You can start your account with a minimum of £250 and trade EUR/USD with a little as 0.6pips and 0.5 size. For Crude Oil the minimum size is 0.25.

CMC Markets

As an easy to use online platform, however the minimum spreads of EUR/USD is 0.7 making it a little expensive.

OANDA

More expensive spreads that CMC and IG stating at 1.3 pips for EUR/USD and 1.1 for USD/JPY.

London Capital Group or LCG

This is among the best forex broker in the UK; however, the starting spreads of EUR/USD is 1.0, more expensive than IG and CMC Markets.

XTB

You can start your account with little as $250 and the standard spreads start from 0.9 pips.

Forex.com

If you have a limited budget, this is the ideal broker because you can start an account with only $50, however the spreads start at 1.3 pips, making it expensive in long run.

Pepperstone

This is a new broker and there a limited review about this broker and I personally have not used, so I am limited to comment about this forex broker. They advertise that their spreads start at 0.0pips which means is market order. And you can start an account with $200 AUD.

ABOUT THE AUTHOR

Smit Chacha has a BSc. Degree in Computer Visualization
and Games and he is an experienced Forex Trader and
author of the popular and famous blog -
http://forextechnicalfundamentals.com/

www.ingramcontent.com/pod-product-compliance
Lightning Source LLC
Chambersburg PA
CBHW030553220526
45463CB00007B/3076